ADHD

What Every Parent Should Know

Alan M. Davick, M.D.

ADHD: What Every Parent Should Know
© 2016 Alan M. Davick, M.D.
ISBN: 978-0-9890053-8-8

MISKIDDING, LLC
P.O. Box 101127
Cape Coral, FL 33910-1127
URL: www.DrDavick.com
Email: miskidding1@gmail.com

Cover Photograph:
© Oxlock | Dreamstime.com
Cover Design: Rik@PublishingSuccessOnline.com

Acknowledgments

Many of the principles presented in this book are distilled from *Managing Misbehavior in Kids: The MIS/Kidding® Process* and from *Discipline Your Child without Going to Jail,* published separately by this author. They were developed by the author over many years with the painstaking collection of expertise from colleagues in the fields of Medicine, Psychology and Education as well as from interaction with innumerable families. To all of those colleagues and families, a hearty thank you!

The author must mention his gratitude to Rik Feeney, author, editor, publisher and coach. His friendship, unfailing professionalism and ready advice has made the writing of this book and its predecessors a pleasure.

And, yet again, to my wife, Barbara, whose early morning refrain, "Are you almost done?" has been heard innumerable times during the writing of this book!

Al Davick

Table of Contents

ADHD: What Every Parent Should Know

Preface

In the late '60's, when I was training as a Pediatrician and later, training as a Behavioral-Developmental Pediatrician, the condition now known as ADHD was termed Minimal Brain Dysfunction (MBD).

We were taught that poorly defined parts of the brains of affected children failed to sort and prioritize incoming stimuli from the environment or even from the child's own brain. This was said to account for affected children's inability to remain on task and even for such bizarre behavior as some children's almost random utterances, sounding as if several thoughts were being expressed simultaneously. Indeed, some children with MBD communicated at times as if they were insane.

Because children with MBD often had a history of distressed pregnancies, prematurity or harmful events during early months or years of life (like breathing problems in the nursery or meningitis), or a family history of multiple close relatives with MBD, the theory held that subtle brain injury or inheritance could create the condition. Lending credibility to this idea was the observation that MBD rarely traveled alone; that is, heritable conditions like mental retardation, bipolar disorder, autism and many genetic disorders often accompanied MBD. Additionally, clumsiness (problems with large and small muscle control), though not reaching a level diagnostic of cerebral palsy, was an additional accompaniment of MBD.

If the diagnostic criteria for MBD[1] were not muddled enough, psychiatrists suspected stress could also mimic the condition, since with the resolution of stress some children with MBD left their symptoms behind.

As time went on, criteria for diagnosing children with intrusive degrees of impulsivity and distractibility, either with or without extreme fidgetiness or "hyperactivity", were agreed upon. During my years of training and medical practice, the name of the condition morphed from MBD to Attention Deficit Disorder with or without Hyperactivity – ADD or ADHD. Throughout this book, I refer to all forms of this condition as ADHD.

The required age of onset of symptoms for a diagnosis of ADHD was extended from 7 years of age through the adult years, both because the condition was often unrecognized, especially when performance was depressed without behavioral issues, and because its symptoms could change from one year to another. Many adults, having early in their lives concluded they were not very bright, were shocked to discover they had suffered from childhood with ADD and that the condition could have been effectively treated before an assault on self-esteem had occurred.

Most recently, psychiatrists have agreed upon diagnostic criteria for ADHD which take into account the fact that the onset of symptoms of ADHD varies from one person to another and from year to year. The latest criteria for diagnosing ADHD are presented in the American Psychiatric Association's Diagnostic and Statistical Manual of Mental

Disorders, 5th edition[2]. The criteria cluster around 2 essential components of ADHD – inattentiveness and hyperactivity. More criteria must be met for the diagnosis below 17 years of age and fewer above that age. ADHD may or may not include hyperactivity. The onset of symptoms must have occurred by 12 years of age, must be intrusive, must not be limited to only one environment and cannot be explained by other psychiatric or neurological conditions.

As you can see, even the latest "simplified" recipe for diagnosing ADHD can be complicated for parents and professionals.

This book is not written as a diagnostic treatise. Rather, it is focused on presenting basic principles parents can understand and use to decide if symptoms they are observing in their child warrant intervention, whether the symptoms are willful or caused by an underlying medical or psychiatric disorder, whether the disorder might qualify as ADHD and, if so, what forms of intervention might be required. A chapter is devoted to acquainting parents with most of the medications use to manage ADHD and a chapter to stopping the treatment of ADHD.

To better understand the focus of this book, let's revisit a bit of the history of ADHD in the Introduction to follow. We'll see what has become clearer with the passage of time is ADHD is not a willful form of misbehavior. Children don't choose to suffer with this condition at the intrusive level of a disorder and they cannot choose to make the disorder go away without treatment. Another way of saying this is discipline doesn't work for children whose ADHD is uncontrolled.

References:

1. Clements SD, Peters JE. Minimal Brain Dysfunction. NINDB Monograph No. 3. Washington: US Public Health Service, 1966

2. American Psychiatric Association: Diagnostic and Statistical Manual of Mental Disorders, 5th edition. Arlington, VA., American Psychiatric Association, 2013.

Introduction

ADHD has a long and interesting history. As a diagnosis, the condition was first referred to as "A Defect in Moral Control"[1] in 1902 by an English physician, Dr. George Still. Affected children exhibited extreme impulsivity, causing them to act out almost any thought entering their consciousness without considering its consequences. This resulted in the random breaking of rules. Affected children found it difficult to engage in consistently respectful discussion with parents or other authorities. They would blurt out any oppositional thought, often in the crudest of terms.

Children with this condition found it almost impossible to contain their activities within safe boundaries. Distractibility led them to flit from one thought to another, from one activity to another. This, in turn, blocked their performance of stepwise tasks and led to poor academic performance, often masking average or above average abilities.

To observers of these behaviors, it often seemed these children had no moral compass to guide them, hence the designation "A Defect in Moral Control."

Many odd observations were generated over the years. For example, hyperactive children were noted to spend extended periods of time playing with and listening to running tap water. During those minutes, even hours, hyperactivity disappeared!

As an interesting aside, scientists postulating a calming effect from the "white noise" of running water, briefly persuaded educators to play recordings of white noise in classrooms and even to arrange "open spaces" in schools, where the sounds of many children and teachers speaking and otherwise interacting could be heard by all. The hope was these efforts would lead to higher levels of concentration for both teachers and students. Unfortunately, performance declined for all concerned, disproving the theory. And teachers, themselves, unable to concentrate, cordoned off the open spaces to contain the noise!

During the late 1930's, Charles Bradley, a psychiatrist, administered Benzedrine, a stimulant medication, to children suffering with headaches who also exhibited a Defect in Moral Control. Much to his surprise, impulsivity, distractibility and hyperactivity improved during the action period of the medication. When the medicine's effects wore off, symptoms returned in full force.

Unfortunately, side effects were observed with the use of Benzedrine, including rapid heart rate, diminished appetite and excessive emotionality. However, Dr. Bradley's observations were not lost on fellow psychiatrists, researchers and drug companies. With the demonstration a stimulant medication could paradoxically control hyperactivity, focus was directed toward manipulating the chemical structure of Benzedrine to improve its effectiveness and decrease its side effects. Soon methylphenidate (Ritalin), dextroamphetamine (Dexedrine) and many other chemical relatives were born.

As chemists were producing an ever growing number of stimulant medications, neurobiologists, physiologists and psychiatrists were utilizing technological discoveries to view the inner workings of the brain. The role of neurotransmitters (chemical messengers in the brain) and the locations of brain structures responsible for "normal" and ADHD behaviors began to emerge.

In recent years, advances in the understanding of brain function in ADHD have expanded treatment options. Now available are non-stimulant medications, most of which escape some or all of the side effects of stimulants, though they have their own potential ill effects.

Today, though much still remains to be discovered, physicians have reliable criteria for the identification of children and adults with ADHD and an array of treatment options and reasonable guidelines for starting or stopping treatment.

So where do parents fit in, given the need for physicians to diagnose and prescribe for ADHD? This book is written to answer that question. Indeed, if you're a parent, this book should be viewed as a guide to the employment of a physician to diagnose and treat suspected ADHD in your child. Yes, you're the employer and the physician is your employee. As with any employee, due diligence (a determination of qualifications, experience, history of success or failure, communication skills) is your responsibility before "hiring" the physician as is "firing" the physician if progress is too slow or non-existent.

This book will enable you to:

- determine if your child has any disorder suggestive of ADHD.
    - ○ No need to go any further if there's no disorder!
- establish treatment goals.
    - ○ You'll need these to judge how well your physician-employee is doing treating the disorder.
- recognize common pitfalls in your physician's treatment of ADHD.
    - ○ You're not the doctor, but you can read and ask questions.
- know when to discipline your child with ADHD.
- know when to stop treating ADHD.

References:

1. Morbid Defect in Moral Control: George Still, Lancet, 1902

2. Bradley C. The Behavior of Children Receiving Benzedrine. Am J Psychiatry. 1937;94:577–581

Glossary of Terms

A defect in moral control: Earliest label for ADHD.

MBD: Minimal Brain Damage – a later historical label for ADHD.

ADD: Attention Deficit Disorder, characterized by inattentiveness, inability to perform sequential tasks and distractibility, consistently intruding on critical life functions.

ADH: Tendencies toward fidgetiness, distractibility and impulsivity not reaching the level of a disability.

ADHD: Attention Deficit Disorder with Hyperactivity

Critical life functions for children: Things children must do to avoid the diagnosis of a disorder.

- Physical: Control of body functions at an appropriate level for age.
- Social: Relate to and benefit from interactions with others at a level appropriate for age, including following reasonable rules.
- Academic: Comprehend and perform schoolwork at an age appropriate level.

Discipline: For children - an instructional process in which children are taught to accept and anticipate consequences for behavioral choices. ADHD disrupts children's ability to think ahead to consequences, thus blocking effective discipline.

Disorder: In the field of child mental health, a "disorder" may be defined as a condition disrupting normal behavior, and observed as one or more of the following:

- Failure to achieve at a level consistent with ability
- Inability to comply with reasonable rules
- Inability to relate beneficially to others

Mania: A psychiatric term referring to a heightened state of excitement and often including hyperactivity of body and mind. Frequently confused with the hyperactivity of ADHD, sometimes treated inappropriately with ADHD medications.

"Horizontal" measure of performance: Judging the normalcy of children's performance by comparing their level of achievement to averages for their age.

"Vertical" measure of performance: Judging the normalcy of children's performance by comparing their level of achievement to their own ability level.

Professionals: People with special knowledge about children and their misbehavior who can help parents with behavioral disorders:

- Physicians: Medical doctors who examine and treat physical problems by doing lab tests, prescribing medicines, doing surgery or hospitalizing children.
- Pediatricians: Medical doctors trained to care for physically ill and well children through 18 (rarely 21) years of age. They are able to prescribe medications, perform minor surgery and hospitalize children.

- Behavioral-Developmental Pediatricians: Medical doctors trained as pediatricians with additional training in mental health and behavioral disorders and disorders of brain development. They are able to prescribe medications, perform minor surgery and hospitalize children
- Child psychiatrists: Medical doctors trained to diagnose and treat mental disorders in children. They are able to prescribe medication and hospitalize children, but rarely perform physical examinations or perform minor surgery.
- Psychologists: Professionals who measure intelligence and assess emotion using standardized psychological tests and who provide counseling and psychotherapy.
- Educators: Professionals primarily concerned with academic performance and who have access to special schools and curricula.

Chapter One

When to suspect ADHD

Does Your Child Have a Disorder?

The last "D" of ADHD – disorder – is the key to deciding if your child has a need for treatment. Before attempting to pin down a suspicion of ADHD, you must first decide if your child is acting normally. A pattern of abnormal behavior in childhood qualifies as a disorder. Of course, there are many forms and causes of abnormal behavior and they are responsible for innumerable disorders beside ADHD. But the core principal to remember is normal behavior eliminates any need for diagnosis or treatment. Consistently normal behavior allows you to stop looking for ADHD. So, what is normal behavior?

Lots of parents and many rebellious teenagers object to the idea of "normal" behavior. They cling to the false premise that everyone's right to individuality obliterates any definition of normal behavior. One teenager exclaimed, "No one can tell me if what I do is normal. I don't want to be your definition of normal!"

Actually, like it or not, society imposes definitions of normal and abnormal behavior on children. Children's abnormal behavior results in societal consequences to the children, some of which include the imposition of restraints by authorities, treatment strategies by professionals (occasionally employing force, against the children's wills) and often punishments by parents. To parents who want their children to be free spirits and to teens who wish to define their own "normal," society responds with certain minimal demands, which when unmet, authorize and fuel consequences, often unpleasant in nature. To remain free to express individuality and fend off unpleasant consequences, children must exhibit a minimum definition of normal behavior.

In its simplest form, normal behavior can be defined by three parameters. Each parameter must be exhibited consistently; that is, most of the time and in most places:

- Performing critical life functions at a level consistent with ability.
- Abiding by reasonable rules.
- Getting along well enough with others that complaints from others are minimal and non-intrusive for the child and the child's family.

Let's look at each of these components of normal behavior a bit more closely.

Performing critical life functions at a level consistent with ability.

Critical life functions for children include physical skills, social skills and academic skills and the criteria for normal performance in each skill area and at each age have been well defined by professionals and are available to all parents[1].

Physicians have defined normal physical skills for children of any age. If parents cannot decide whether their children's physical skills are up to par, they can employ a physician to examine their children for a definitive answer.

Psychologists have defined normal social skills for children of all ages. When parents cannot decide if their children's social skills are normal, they can employ a psychologist to make a definitive determination.

Educators have defined age-appropriate academic performance for children of all ages. Grade levels of achievement are roughly reported each school year, though when parents question their accuracy, additional individualized testing by educators or psychologists will procure definitive results.

Children who consistently exhibit a pattern of failure to perform critical life functions qualify as exhibiting a disorder, though its specific identity may not yet have been determined.

Children who successfully perform critical life functions at a level consistent with ability, the first of three parameters of normal behavior, may still suffer with a disorder if they cannot abide by reasonable rules.

Abiding by reasonable rules.
This second measure of normal behavior is judged by the authorities in a child's life. Unlike the criteria for normal critical life skills, all of which have been measured and published by professionals, normality in abiding by reasonable rules is a matter of opinion. Those judging the following of rules include not only parents, brothers, sisters and relatives, but individuals outside the home, such as teachers, principals, policemen, bus drivers, playmates and schoolmates. Nonetheless, in any society there is a core of critical rules with an expectation they'll be followed. Surrounding the core of

critical rules are more arbitrary (non-critical) rules some authorities, including parents, may wish to impose. A wise parent or authority will impose fewer and fewer arbitrary rules on children who are growing in maturity and who are accepting responsibility for their acts. This is the key to minimizing conflict with children over rules.

Critical rules are considered important by almost everyone. For example, trying to stab a parent or teacher with a pencil or a knife would be considered rule-breaking and abnormal behavior by nearly any parent or teacher, especially as a recurring pattern of behavior. By contrast, children picking their noses at the dinner table is not universally accepted as the breaking of a "reasonable" rule – (as an experienced practitioner, I will attest to this!).

In general, children engaged in a pattern of consistently breaking core critical rules qualify as exhibiting a disorder, though its specific identity may not yet have been determined.

Avoiding a pattern of complaints from others.

The last measure of abnormal behavior is also the most subjective of the parameters of a disorder. In the last analysis, parents must decide if complaints from others about their child are frequent enough and intrusive enough to define their children's behavior as abnormal.

When parents identify complaints from others as the only evidence of possibly abnormal behavior, without their children failing to perform critical life functions and without the breaking of rules, their children may or may not have a disorder.

Complaints generated by parents, but no one else, suggest those parents are imposing too many arbitrary rules. If the parents simply abandoned those (unnecessary?) rules, they would eliminate any need for further investigation. Complaints originating outside the family, especially if they are numerous, do suggest abnormal behavior and the presence of a disorder.

If as a parent you've applied these measures to your child and have identified consistently abnormal behavior, you've exposed a disorder. Some disorders are characterized by willful defiance, representing poor decision-making by otherwise capable children. Such disorders respond to discipline. Other disorders block children from behaving well. These disorders don't respond to discipline, since discipline requires children to organize their thinking and look ahead to consequences. ADHD belongs to this second category. Uncontrolled, it's characterized by impulsivity and disorganized thinking which block effective discipline.

Meet Alaina. She has a disorder responsive to discipline.

Alaina was 10 years old when her Mom brought her to my office and explained she and her husband separated last year and live in different homes. Alaina lived with Mom, but spent every other weekend with Dad. Mom complained Alaina was bullying 2 neighboring children whenever she saw them. Their parents had complained repeatedly to Mom and even threatened to call the police. At Mom's home, when Alaina was asked to bathe, prepare to meet the school bus in the mornings or clean her room, she responded with anger, even hitting. Mom was especially frustrated by Dad's description of ideal behavior on Alaina's part at his home.

After spending some time with Alaina, her Mom and later, her Dad, it became clear Alaina's anger over the separation of her parents was targeting Mom, though Mom was neither abusive nor neglectful. Alaina was able to "turn a switch" on and off, depending on which parent she was with. Clearly, she had control over the expression of her anger.

Alaina's mental health diagnoses included Oppositional Defiant Disorder (ODD) and Adjustment Disorder (also called Stress Response Syndrome). Neither of these disorders are "built in" to the brain. Neither is due to abnormal brain chemistry or inheritance. Both are examples of mental health conditions responsive to discipline.*

This family's problem was solved by referral to a therapist who helped Alaina's parents construct a disciplinary strategy. The essence of the strategy was based on Dad's doling out of affection to Alaina for right behavior at Mom's home. Mom became Dad's "eyes" in her home.

* In this book, discipline refers to a process of instruction, utilizing affection to encourage right behavior. It does not refer to painful or punitive responses to poor choice-making. Affection, honestly earned, builds self-esteem, punishment generates anger or depression.

Now, meet Dontae. He has a disorder unresponsive to discipline.

Dontae was 17 years old when he came to my office with his parents. After several years of worsening rages, Dontae had assaulted another student at school and was arrested. A Court appearance was pending.

After several sessions with Dontae and his parents, a frightening picture emerged. The parents related their son had always had a short temper. But in the last several years, Dontae's physical size and the intensity of his anger had resulted in property damage and, more recently, serious injuries to others. It seemed even trivial provocations, like being asked to clean his room or turn off his cell phone in class, resulted in rages.

Dontae acknowledged his emotions could change suddenly, intensely and often without any identifiable trigger. This mood cycling included periods of hyperactivity and reckless behavior, but also periods of depression and sluggishness.

After several sessions with Dontae, a diagnosis of Bipolar Disorder was established. Several other blood relatives on both sides of his family had also been diagnosed with this condition.

Dontae required several medications to control his Bipolar Disorder. He agreed to engage in therapy to learn how to defuse anger flare-ups in their earliest stages. His Court appearance resulted in a period of mandatory community service.

Bipolar Disorder does not respond to discipline alone. It's an example of an abnormality of brain chemistry and it can be inherited from other generations.

Tell Me Again...How Do I Recognize a Disorder?

Remember, normal behavior can be defined by three parameters. Each must be exhibited consistently; that is, most of the time and in most places:

- Performing critical life functions at a level consistent with ability.
- Abiding by reasonable rules.
- Getting along well enough with others that complaints from others are minimal and non-intrusive for the child and the child's family.

OK, My Child Has a Disorder – Could It Be ADHD?

The next step in confirming a suspicion of ADHD is to move forward from the last "D" in ADHD to the "H". Does your child exhibit hyperactivity? Answering this question is not as simple as you might think. In deciding if a child has the hyperactivity of ADHD, several other conditions mimicking ADHD need to be identified if present and managed or eliminated. Recall Dontae's story. He exhibited hyperactivity, but turned out to have Bipolar Disorder. Had he been treated for ADHD, his symptoms would have worsened, possibly to a life-endangering level. On the next pages, I've listed some disorders which are often confused with ADHD.

Diagnosing ADHD typically requires the assistance of one or more physicians, possibly including a pediatrician, a child neurologist or a child psychiatrist.

This book is not written to enable parents to diagnose ADHD or any of its associated disorders. Rather, the focus is on acquainting parents with the steps they need to take to procure recognition and effective treatment of the condition. As the employers of consulting professionals, parents need to be able to judge if those professionals are taking the necessary steps to resolve the disorder. Consultants who fail to consider critical steps should be fired and replaced.

Some Disorders Mimic "Hyperactivity," but are Not ADHD.

Each of the disorders in the following list can mimic the hyperactivity of ADHD, but require treatment other than that usually prescribed for ADHD. Each has been observed and treated by the author during more than 40 years of practice. Each requires professional assistance for recognition and treatment. In the author's experience, specific therapy for each listed disorder improves or eliminates the hyperactivity, while typical therapy for ADHD, if prescribed in error, rarely resolves the symptom and may worsen it. None of the listed conditions eliminates the possibility of coexisting ADHD. As one of the author's mentors once quipped, "Children can have as many diseases as they pleases!"

To be effective employees for parents, professionals chosen to consider the diagnosis and treatment of ADHD must be familiar with and explore the possible existence or co-existence of the following disorders.

For each listed condition, one or more professional consultants are suggested:

Watch Out for these Disorders Masquerading as ADHD.

Name of Disorder	Typical Symptoms	Professional
Adjustment Disorder -a reaction to stress	Depression Anger Hyperactivity	Child Psychiatrist
Anemia -decreased oxygen delivery	Lack of stamina Hyperactivity	Pediatrician Hematologist
Autism -abnormal use of language, deficient social skills	Deficient social skills Stereotyped routines Hyperactivity	Child Psychologist Child Psychiatrist
Bipolar Disorder -mental disorder affecting stamina, mood, behavior and sleep	Mood instability Depression Manic episodes (often confused w/ hyperactivity)	Child Psychiatrist
Hearing Loss	Inability to follow verbal directions Hyperactivity	Pediatrician Audiologist
Hyperthyroidism -overactive thyroid gland	Weight loss Heart palpitations Hyperactivity	Pediatrician Endocrinologist

Hypoglycemia *-low blood sugar*	Irritability Sleepiness/Inattentiveness Hyperactivity	Pediatrician Endocrinologist
Sensory Integration Disorder *-abnormal brain processing*	Oversensitivity to sensations / Hyperactivity	Pediatric Neurologist
Sleep Apnea *-periodic cessation of breathing during sleep*	High red blood cell count Irritability/Moodiness Hyperactivity	Pediatric Neurologist
Toxins • Flavorings • Colorings • Heavy metals • Food allergies	Rashes Signs of brain damage Loss of previously acquired skills Hyperactivity	Pediatrician
Vital Organ Disease *-nervous system, heart, lungs, kidneys, glands, liver, etc.*	May cause poor focus with without hyperactivity	Pediatrician
Vitamin/Mineral Deficiencies *-may affect almost any bodily function*	Lack of stamina Poor focus Irritability Hyperactivity	Pediatrician Nutritionist

The symptom of hyperactivity as a component of ADHD almost always announces its presence in school – often in preschool, though parents may recognize its intrusive consequences at home within the first two years of life. It is always annoying and may be dangerous.

Annoyance with children exhibiting the hyperactivity of ADHD may be created by a frequent need to replace babysitters who become exasperated by the children's behavior, but also by complaints from storekeepers who see products falling from shelves and items briefly held and misplaced and, in school aged children, notes from teachers whose classes are repeatedly disrupted.

Hyperactivity is almost always accompanied by impulsivity; that is, affected children tend to act on any thought entering their minds before considering consequences. Many young children with ADHD have awakened in early morning hours, rushed out of bed, unlocked doors and stumbled into pools, there to drown before anyone discovered they had left the home.

As annoying and potentially dangerous as hyperactivity may be, the remaining components of ADHD, impulsivity, distractibility and inability to organize and perform multistep tasks, intrude most predictably on critical life functions.

Could My Child Have ADD (with or without "H")?

In 2013, the American Psychiatric Association published its Diagnostic and Statistical Manual of Mental Disorders, 5th edition[2] in which revised criteria for the diagnosis of ADHD were presented to mental health practitioners. The criteria were expanded to include diagnosis in adults, though onset of symptoms were required in childhood.

Two broad groups of symptoms were required; inattentiveness/distractibility and hyperactivity/impulsivity. Symptoms were required to occur in several locations rather than being restricted, for example, to the home. This is an important concept because children who limit abnormal behavior solely to one or another locale are turning a behavioral switch "on" or "off" at will, thus demonstrating a degree of decision-making incompatible with ADHD.

Symptoms also had to intrude significantly on critical areas of performance and could not be otherwise explained by alternate disorders, such as those listed above.

In spite of these revisions, the diagnosis of ADHD remains a subjective process for professionals. No single diagnostic test can be relied upon for the diagnosis. This means any professional employed by a parent to evaluate, diagnose and treat ADHD is best chosen after careful consideration of training and experience, as would be true for the hiring of any employee.

Parents should suspect the possibility of ADD as a diagnosis whenever their children cannot consistently perform tasks in sequence and ADHD when hyperactivity accompanies behavior suggestive of ADD.

Now let's see how parents can initiate and manage an investigation of their child's disorder to eliminate or diagnose and treat ADHD.

References:

1. Managing Misbehavior in Kids: The MIS/Kidding Process, AM Davick, 206-207, Mis/kidding, L.L.C., 2014.

2. American Psychiatric Association: Diagnostic and Statistical Manual of Mental Disorders, 5th edition. Arlington, VA., American Psychiatric Association, 2013.

Chapter Two

How to start and manage an investigation for ADHD

In the preceding chapter, we learned to suspect a disorder whenever we encountered consistently abnormal behavior. We defined abnormal behavior as failure to exhibit any one or more of the following parameters:

- Performing critical life functions at a level consistent with ability.
- Abiding by reasonable rules.
- Getting along well enough with others that complaints from others are minimal and non-intrusive for the child and the child's family.

Within the first parameter, we learned critical life functions for children included physical, social and academic skills. We recognized these skill areas as the domains of physicians, psychologists and educators.

Parents know their children best. They are able to discern their children's failure to perform in one or more of these critical skill areas. But, in initiating an investigation of suspected disorders for a child, parents must be prepared for the possibility professional consultants may expose several unsuspected conditions, some of which mimic ADHD.

Because many disorders can mimic ADHD, an organized approach to the investigation is required to ensure accurate and effective treatment. Backtracking after "firing" one or more consultants is costly, time-consuming and stressful for both children and parents.

Deciding Which Professional Consultants to Hire.

Over the years, I've found choosing the best professional consultant to begin investigating a possible disorder, including ADHD, is to begin with the assessment of a child's physical competence by a physician. For children, it's best to begin with a pediatrician. Pediatricians are medical doctors trained to care for healthy and sick children.

Behavioral-Developmental Pediatricians are pediatricians who have acquired additional training in neurology, child psychiatry and genetics and who focus on diagnosing and treating children with disorders affecting performance and behavior. They are most often found in or near regional medical centers where they serve children referred to them by primary care physicians, including pediatricians.

What pediatricians and developmental-behavioral pediatricians do for ADHD.

Pediatricians and developmental-behavioral pediatricians begin by reviewing the family's history of medical conditions to identify risks. They must rule out any process potentially causing ongoing damage, such as brain degeneration, lead poisoning or an overactive thyroid gland. Medicines taken for other reasons may contribute to or even cause ADHD. Associated neurological conditions, like Tourette disorder, cerebral palsy or epilepsy and associated psychiatric disorders, like bipolar disorder, need to be identified and treated.

An example of hyperactivity caused by a medicine.

Jose, 7 years of age, was brought to my office on referral from his pediatrician. He was having difficulty keeping up with his 2nd grade class and was described by his teacher as "being in constant motion," frequently disrupting the class. His pediatrician suspected Jose of having ADHD.

Before his arrival in my office, Jose had been referred to an endocrinologist (gland doctor) for obesity. He had just begun taking thyroid hormone for an underactive thyroid condition and was rapidly thinning down, to his family's delight.

In speaking with the family and comparing school observations from 1st and 2nd grade, it seemed Jose's behavior had changed from normal to abnormal with the start of his thyroid medication. A simple blood test confirmed Jose's thyroid hormone dose was higher than it needed to be. When the dose was lowered, the ADHD-like symptoms quickly disappeared. No other treatment was required.

The pediatrician may next gather observations from teachers and family members to compare the child's behaviors in different settings. This should pin down the requirement for a diagnosis of ADHD that the child does not switch abnormal behavior "on" and "off" depending on location.

Physical and neurological examinations usually follow the history-taking. Laboratory tests may be performed. It's at this point conditions mimicking ADHD will be recognized.

An example of a scary and dangerous condition mimicking ADHD.

Lala, age 4 years, was referred to my office after her preschool observed extreme hyperactivity and developmental delay. Lela had just moved to the U.S. from India with her parents. By her parents' description, Mom's pregnancy had been healthy as had been Lala's first 3 years of life. During the family's preparation for their move to the U.S., Lala had begun exhibiting odd movements of her arms and legs, irritability and increasingly intrusive hyperactivity. Of greatest concern was Lala's loss of coordination during the past few months. Lala's preschool reported she was barely functioning at the 3 year level.

After a battery of blood tests were completed, Lala was discovered to have a toxic blood lead level. She required hospitalization and extensive detoxification. Though her hyperactivity and deterioration stopped, she continued to show signs of brain damage long after her lead poisoning was reversed. Lala's heavy metal exposure was eventually shown to have been caused by lead-contaminated candy her parents gave her during their stressful move to the U.S.

Your pediatrician may discover specific physical conditions contributing to abnormal behavior. If so, referral to a pediatric specialist might be required. Brain and nervous system conditions may require consultation with a pediatric neurologist. Gland-related problems may require assistance from a pediatric endocrinologist. Each organ system has specialists who can investigate further. Because the investigation of physical conditions can become complex and costly and because your pediatrician is the "captain" of the professional team, the choice of a trusted pediatrician is a critical decision. Here's how to find a good pediatrician (or other child specialist).

How to hire a physician.

You may have heard the joke, "What do they call the medical student who graduates with the lowest grades in his class?" The answer: "Doctor!" Though meant as a joke, the truth is not all doctors have the same capabilities.

To increase the odds physicians you hire to investigate your suspicion of ADHD do a good job, you need to consider their competence and their ability to communicate with you.

Judging the competence of a physician.

Judging the competence of a physician can seem like an insurmountable obstacle to a parent. Actually, in this Internet Age, there are many helpful and reliable resources to accomplish this task.

Begin with two basic measures of competence – licensing and lawsuits. Physicians must meet certain federal and state requirements while continuing to stay up-to-date on new medical knowledge in order to be relicensed at periodic intervals. Reports of these achievements are public knowledge. Serious (and sometimes not-so-serious) disagreements with patients and bad outcomes resulting in lawsuits are monitored and also made public. Documentation of these basic measures can most easily be found and examined on the American Medical Association website: http://www.ama-assn.org.

Judging how well a physician communicates.

This test begins with a parent's first encounter with the physician. Parents must judge how easy or difficult it is to reach the physician, either in person with an appointment, or by phone. Credit is given for off-hours accessibility and weekend availability. Demerits are subtracted for being shunted off to receptionist after receptionist, answering services during standard hours or being required to rehash basic facts with a nurse or physician's assistant in lieu of the physician.

Parents will want to know whether their physician agrees to advise them of critical lab results in a timely fashion and whether copies of their child's consults and lab tests will be made readily available to them as well as to other physicians working with the child. Failure to make results available to critical parties, including parents, is like not having completed the consultation at all, though parents can anticipate they'll be charged for such non-service.

Parents need to be sure their physician is willing to explain in advance the strategy and anticipated steps that will be taken to answer the question, "Is my child willfully misbehaving or does he have a condition forcing him to act this way?" To glean this information from a physician, parents need to ask, "How do you plan to go about finding out if my child has an underlying condition causing this misbehavior? How long will it take to get answers? Will you tell me when and if you think we'll need to consult other physicians before doing so?"

Finally, likeability contributes to successful communication. Speaking with others, when possible, who have consulted a proposed physician consultant is always helpful. Although several search engines on the Internet report patient satisfaction surveys and even score physicians on many above-mentioned parameters, keep in mind patients with complaints tend to record their experiences while those with positive experiences are rarely motivated to do so. Thus a scattering of negative comments on a public website is rarely a reliable resource.

Remember, the fruits of competence without effective communication are expense without usable results.

After the physical component of critical life functions has been assessed by physician(s), any failure to perform within the social or academic skill areas will need to be measured and defined by a psychologist. When a child's comprehension is deficient, learning disabilities are present or autistic behavior is exhibited, it is the psychologist who will best define the disorder.

What child psychologists do for ADHD.

Child psychologists measure levels of ability in the many areas of intelligence, the degree to which achievement of age-appropriate skills has occurred, the intensity and healthfulness of emotionality and the extent to which children can understand and accept limits.

After ability, achievement levels, emotionality, comprehension and acceptance of limits have been measured and compared to norms, experienced child psychologists help parents, teachers and physicians develop reasonable behavioral expectations: At what grade level does the child comprehend schoolwork? How well can the child understand the behavior of adults, friends and family? At what age level can the child be expected to follow rules? And, by answering these questions, the psychologist provides a basis for effective discipline of willful misbehavior, like defiance.

Included within formal psychological testing are measures of inattentiveness, distractibility and inability to adequately perform sequential tasks – the diagnostic criteria for ADD. Among the various child professionals, the child psychologist is best equipped to reliably diagnose ADD.

Some children may require psychotherapy, medication or both to create or increase their ability to anticipate rewards and punishments as the consequence of behavioral choices. Children's ability to anticipate the consequences of their behavioral choices is critical to effective discipline.

Still other children may need such treatment for previously unrecognized depression, including family therapy to manage or eliminate relational stresses.

Distinct from child psychologists (no M.D. degree), child psychiatrists (with M.D. degree) are best consulted when medication is indicated or psychiatric hospitalization is required for associated mental disorders.

Most children with untreated ADHD find it difficult or impossible to achieve consistently at the level of their ability as determined by psychological testing. With appropriate treatment, the hurdle of ADHD is removed, and children can achieve at the level of their true competence.

Psychological testing - a critical need to determine realistic goals for a child.

Naji, age 10 years, was brought to my office by his grandparents (his guardians) as he was about to repeat 3rd grade for a third time, though in a class for children with behavioral problems. His pediatrician suspected ADHD as a cause of his academic delays.

Naji had been removed from his parents' care soon after birth, having experienced cocaine withdrawal symptoms in the nursery as a result of his Mom's addiction. His physical health had been good thereafter, but sitting, walking and speech development had all been delayed. Nevertheless, Naji's friendly demeanor and social skills resulted in his placement in age-appropriate 1st and 2nd grade classes at school.

As time went on and Naji fell further behind his classmates, teachers began to observe Naji wandering from desk to desk and out into the hallways. At times, he would act the class clown, disrupting class activities and necessitating his removal to the principal's office. Teacher Observation Scales listed inattentiveness, distractibility, impulsivity and hyperactivity as worrisome behaviors – all suggestive of ADHD.

During a session with Naji's grandparents, they indicated Naji tended to play with younger children in the neighborhood. Indeed, they judged Naji's behaviors were more like those of two, 6-year-old, 1st-grade neighbor children.

With the grandparents' approval, we proceeded to petition Naji's school psychologist to perform formal psychometric testing (measures of IQ, achievement, social maturity and emotionality). The tests revealed Mild Mental Retardation, though social skills were close to normal for Naji's age. His social maturity had led his guardians, his teachers and even his pediatrician to overestimate his academic ability levels.

As a result of his psychological tests, Naji was placed in a Special Education program at a level consistent with his ability. His ADHD symptoms soon disappeared.

Finding the right psychologist to assess your child for ADHD and associated mental disorders can be confusing due to the many "species" of psychologists available. Here are some guidelines to follow:

How to choose and manage a psychologist.

Although all psychologists are familiar with ADHD, some "species" of psychologists are more proficient than others at assessing it. For example, psychologists who have reached the doctoral level (i.e. Ph.D.'s) may be expected to have wider experience in testing, counseling and therapy, while Masters level psychologists (i.e. M.A.) likely have greater capabilities than Bachelor level psychologists (i.e. B.A. or B.S.), but less than Ph.D's.

Bachelor level psychologists, often called psychometrists (i.e. "mind-measurers") can reliably administer tests of intelligence (i.e. I.Q. tests), achievement and social maturity, but usually do not have the required training and experience to diagnose mental illness or provide psychotherapy. Psychometrists are often employed by schools to perform tests for the purpose of developing Individualized Educational Plans (i.e. IEP's) and other educational strategies. Because psychometrists wear two hats (advocate for both the school and the child), their recommendations may be influenced more by what services the school has available than strictly by what the child needs.

Doctoral psychologists are more professionally independent than Masters level psychologists or Bachelor level psychologists. This means they can more easily act as a child's advocate, especially if the child requires services not readily available through the school. These highly trained psychologists can measure, interpret and counsel at any level required by their findings.

The differences between school psychologists and private psychologists.

In addition to the different "species" of psychologists outlined above, psychologists may be found in various "habitats." As I've mentioned, lesser trained psychologists are likely to be less independent from their employer (such as a school) than more highly trained psychologists. Parents are more likely to ensure advocacy for their child the more highly trained the psychologist they consult. Even so, school psychologists even at the doctoral level are, by definition, employees of schools and are obligated by their employer to consider the resources and budget of the school when proposing appropriate services for a child. This means their recommendations are likely to be flavored to at least some extent by the school's staffing or budgetary limitations. The result may be a proposal for a less costly service or one for which the school has staffing rather than a more appropriate, though more costly or more staff-intensive service. This conundrum can be avoided by consulting a psychologist in private practice (not employed by a school).

Though private psychologists are not free of cost like school psychologists, their allegiance is directed entirely at the parents who hire them and their child. If parents have doubts about their child's abilities, special needs or performance levels as they are presented by a child's school or are contesting a strategy the school has proposed, they may choose to employ a private, Ph.D.-level clinical child psychologist. This species of independent, highly trained professional, removed from the habitat of the school, can advocate wholly for children and assist parents in formulating the best educational strategies.

Once a child has been diagnosed with ADD or ADHD and any associated conditions identified, accommodated or eliminated, treatment may confidently begin. In the next chapter we'll explore common errors made by parents and professionals in treating ADHD. But first, let's examine the critical role educator's play in the diagnosis and treatment of ADHD.

What educators do for ADHD.

Educators spend more time with children than any other professionals and occasionally more time with them than their parents! Teachers' observations are extremely valuable in identifying ADHD, judging its severity and weighing the effects of treatment on an ongoing basis. All three of children's critical life functions - ability to perform physically, socially and academically, ability to follow reasonable rules and ability to avoid a pattern of complaints from others – are on display in school. Most easily tracked is academic performance.

An example of educators providing critical observations in managing ADHD.

Lovesa, age 5, was referred to my office by her pediatrician. He had been treating her for ADHD with Methylphenidate ER (MPD-ER, Concerta), a stimulant medication. Lovesa had responded well to this medication initially, but had now reached the top recommended dose of medication with re-emergence of ADHD symptoms. Her pediatrician was concerned about potential side effects if the dose were to be increased.

MPD-ER, like all stimulant medications, can cause heart and blood pressure irregularities, loss of appetite, headaches and stomachaches, moodiness and many other less frequent ill effects. There are, however, children who are "fast metabolizers" – individuals who break down medications at a much faster rate than average and who require higher doses of medications to maintain effective blood levels. Lovesa's pediatrician suspected she might be a fast metabolizer of MPD-ER.

In order to safely raise Lovesa's MPD-ER dose above the recommended level, frequent measures of heart and blood pressure effects (vital signs) would be required till an effective response was achieved. Vital signs would be checked at either doctor's office, but judging effective response would require ongoing observations by the educators.

Over a period of several weeks, Lovesa's MPD-ER dose was increased to twice the usual recommended dose. Her vital signs remained completely normal, qualifying her as a fast metabolizer. Teacher Checklists indicated academic performance was dramatically improved, appetite at lunch remained intact and emotionality remained stable.

I saw Lovesa for several months before returning her care to her pediatrician. During that time, on a high dose of MPD-ER, Lovesa's school performance remained above average without the return of ADHD symptoms.

ADHD may affect only one area of learning, such as math, or may affect many areas of learning. Additionally, ADHD is often associated with other disorders, such as speech and language disorders, emotional disorders and intellectual limitation. The performance deficits associated with ADHD can be measured, at no expense to parents, by educators. Here's a list of educators who assess and plan curricula for children with ADHD and associated disabilities:

- Speech and language clinicians and speech pathologists help children overcome unintelligible speech and problems understanding and communicating verbal concepts.
- Special education teachers help children acquire and utilize information with techniques that compensate for their disabilities.
- Perceptual motor specialists help children use their bodies to develop self-help skills, communicate their desires and demonstrate their abilities.
- School psychologists track children's academic and emotional progress, perform tests for comparison to norms and previous levels of achievement and help design Individualized Educational Programs (I.E.P.'s)
- Pupil personnel workers assess the strengths and vulnerabilities of children and their families, helping them to adjust to disabilities and achieve normal behavioral goals.

Teachers are often the first observers to recognize ADD or ADHD. Initial discussion of symptoms by teachers with parents often occurs early in a child's school experience – sometimes in preschool. As descriptions of abnormal behavior increase in number and spill over from one class to another or from one school to another, a parent will begin to recognize the likely presence of a disorder worthy of investigation.

Once a child is diagnosed and begins a treatment strategy for ADHD, the success or failure of the strategy will be observed by teachers. A number of rating scales are available for parents and teachers and can be used to identify ADHD and its response to treatment. One useful online site providing such measures is: www.chadd.org.

Why physician and psychologist evaluations should precede repeating a grade.

One caution worth mentioning, and which will be discussed at greater length later in this book, is the fact that a child's ability is not defined by school performance or grade level of achievement; that is, achievement does not equal capability.

Teachers are trained to measure a child's performance, which is most commonly expressed as a grade level of achievement. Teachers are not trained to administer IQ tests, tests of social maturity or to recognize mental health conditions limiting academic performance. When children with or without ADHD are unable to keep up with others of their age and are held back a grade, schools often rely on repeating a grade to solve the performance problem.

But, untreated ADHD and many other untreated physical and mental disorders don't improve with time. Indeed, their impact on academic performance worsens over time. Without the certainty that physical or mental disorders, including ADHD have been treated or ruled out by physicians and psychologists, repeating grades is a recipe for continued failure.

Now that we've seen how and in what order to hire professionals to assess a suspicion of a disorder – ADHD or any accompanying disorder - let's imagine we've been advised by one or more professionals the diagnosis of ADHD is confirmed. A treatment strategy has been suggested by the pediatrician, child neurologist or child psychiatrist. In the next chapter we'll examine frequent mistakes parents and professionals make in treating ADHD.

Chapter Three

Common errors made in treating ADHD

This chapter is written as a guide for parents of children who have been diagnosed with ADHD. The examples presented are drawn from the author's extensive experience as a consultant to primary care providers and psychiatric colleagues and directly to families whose children have been referred for treatment of this disorder.

It's not uncommon for children with ADHD to have been subjected to many ineffective or even hurtful treatment strategies before successful management of the disorder is eventually achieved. Parents who are aware of potential pitfalls as they or their consultants devise a treatment plan are able to avoid costly or hurtful outcomes. Parents who are so equipped need not act as diagnosticians nor should they assume the role of the specialist. But, by asking critical questions at predictable decision points, they can increase the likelihood of a timely and successful outcome.

The discussion of common errors in this chapter is divided into two major categories – errors parents commonly make and errors professionals commonly make. In each case, a basic principle is presented along with a question to be posed, either self-directed by the child's parent or directed at the treating consultant.

Remember, parents do the hiring and firing of consultants based on success or failure to manage or eliminate the disorder. While technical aspects of the treatment plan, such as psychotherapy and medication management, fall within the domain of the professional, it's appropriate for parents to judge if the treatment plan is advancing in a timely fashion and whether it's effective or not. Hiring a professional to diagnose and treat ADHD is not unlike hiring a plumber to fix a leaky faucet. You may not know how to identify the cause of the leak and how to repair it, but you, as the consumer, know if it's costing too much, taking too long to repair and whether the leak is fixed when the plumber says it is.

Common Errors Parents Make with ADHD

Choosing the wrong professional to make the diagnosis.

Some neurologists, many pediatricians, all behavioral-developmental pediatricians and all child psychiatrists have been trained to evaluate, diagnose and treat ADHD. Though psychologists don't usually diagnose ADHD, formal testing by these professionals can document patterns of performance indicative of ADD and lead you to consult a physician for assessment of this disorder.

Choosing the wrong professional to make or eliminate the diagnosis of ADHD can be costly, time-consuming or even hazardous.

What to ask when choosing a professional to diagnose or treat ADHD: **"Do you have training and experience evaluating and treating children who may have ADHD?"**

Mistaking normal behavior for ADHD.

If you, a grandparent, a teacher, a neighbor or anyone else mentions the suspicion your child has ADHD, recall what you've learned about disorders. Children who are-

- Performing critical life functions at a level consistent with ability, including physical skills, social skills and academic skills,
- Abiding by reasonable rules,
- Getting along well enough with others that complaints from others are minimal and non-intrusive for the child and the child's family,

- do not have a disorder. They may have ADH (without the "D" – that is, merely annoying idiosyncrasies, but no disorder) exhibiting a degree of distractibility, impulsivity, disorganization and fidgetiness qualifying as annoyances, but if these traits don't intrude upon critical life functions they don't require treatment.

What to ask when a suspicion of ADHD is raised: **"Does the child qualify as having a 'disorder'?"**

Answer this question by checking the child's performance in each of the three areas of critical life functions: performance - (physical, social, academic), rule-following and relationships to others.

Failing to repeat achievement testing once ADHD is treated.

Many children with undiagnosed or untreated ADHD are placed in special educational programs designed for those with disruptive behavior. Others may be placed in lower functioning educational programs due to poor academic performance.

Both of these issues may improve dramatically once ADHD is identified and controlled. Children who remain in an inappropriate behavioral program, with lowered academic expectations, often exhibit misbehavior modelled after their classmates, while those remaining in a lower functioning class fall further behind their true peers.

What to ask once ADHD is treated: **"Is my child catching up to his peers? Is he ready to return to a higher functioning class?"**

Failing to measure a child's abilities.

This error often incorporates the above-mentioned error of mistaking normal behavior for ADHD, but also includes the obverse; mistaking abnormal behavior for normal. Some examples will clarify several versions of this error.

An example of unrecognized mental retardation: "Normal" behavior misinterpreted as abnormal behavior.

Juan is 6 years old and is enrolled in a 1st grade class at a local school. His kindergarten teacher last year voiced concerns to Mom about Juan's readiness for 1st grade. He seemed somewhat hyperactive, often intruding on other student's activities, and he rarely completed assigned tasks in spite of one-on-one attention by his teacher. Since he and his family moved from a Spanish-speaking country 2 years ago, some of Juan's difficulties were thought to be due to his incomplete command of English. During the kindergarten year, Juan's language skills improved measurably and his Mom opted to allow him to progress to 1st grade.

This year, Juan seems unable to keep up with his classmates. He darts from one activity and one location in class to another. His behavior is often disruptive and he has been removed from class on occasion when his insatiable curiosity has interrupted his classmates' activities. Juan's teacher has suggested Juan may suffer from ADHD and advises his Mom to seek an assessment.

Mom begins by consulting Juan's pediatrician. When asked by the doctor to estimate Juan's overall level of comprehension, Mom relates Juan seems to perform at about the same level as her 4 year old daughter. The pediatrician recommends formal psychological testing, including measures of IQ. Fortunately, the school agrees to have such testing done by its school psychologist at no expense to the family.

The results of the testing surprise Mom and, to some extent, Juan's teacher. Juan is found to have a mental age of 4 years (corroborating Mom's observations of performance level), equivalent to an IQ of 70. This qualifies Juan for Special Education services in his school. Juan is placed in a special education class and presented with classwork at the 4 year level. Almost immediately, Juan's "abnormal" behaviors, including disruptive intrusions into classmates' activities, hyperactivity and distractibility disappear. Juan, 6 years of age, begins to successfully achieve at the 4 year level, consistent with his measured ability.

This scenario illustrates the common error of failing to identify the cause of diminished comprehension in a child whose behavior seems abnormal for his age. Boredom and frustration related to the child's inability to comprehend and engage with classroom activities leads to apparent hyperactivity, distractibility and intrusiveness, suggesting ADHD. But once the child's mental retardation is defined by formal testing, and appropriate educational programming is achieved, these "normal" signs of frustration and stress by a mentally retarded child disappear and with them the symptoms misinterpreted as ADHD.

An example of unrecognized hearing loss: Abnormal behavior misinterpreted as "normal" behavior.

Alicia is 5 years old and is enrolled in kindergarten. Mom has been advised by an ER physician who treated Alicia for vomiting, diarrhea and dehydration that she probably suffers from ADHD. A child psychiatrist, with whom Mom consulted because of her daughter's odd behaviors, suggested an additional diagnosis of mild autism.

In class and at home, Alicia often hums to herself while engaging in what the psychiatrist termed, "self-stimulatory activities." These include tapping her skull with a finger and smelling objects like erasers and crayons. Her teacher has complained she often wanders about the class in school, ignoring repeated verbal directives by the teacher to remain seated. When spoken to, Alicia usually stops and stares as if in a trance, then continues her inappropriate activities. Alicia has fallen well behind her class and her Mom has been told by the school she will likely have to repeat kindergarten. In discussing Alicia's behaviors with the child psychiatrist, Mom is advised Alicia's behaviors are "normally" seen in autistic children with ADHD.

Fortunately for Alicia, regularly scheduled hearing assessments by the school identify her as a child with severe high-tone hearing loss. She is able to hear mid to low tones, thus being alerted to attempts at verbal communication from parents, teachers and classmates, but she is unable to comprehend content.

Over a period of several months, Alicia's hearing loss is treated with costly and specialized hearing aids. Her attention span improves dramatically while her apparent "hyperactivity" disappears. Her self-stimulatory behaviors also disappear. Though Alicia's behaviors were considered "normal" for a child with ADHD and autism, it soon becomes evident she neither suffers with ADHD nor autism.

An example of a gifted child exhibiting ADHD-like behavior.

Devonta is a six year old first grader who has generated numerous complaints by his teacher. He often leaves his seat during exercises while other students are working, disrupting class activities. He blurts out answers when other students are asked questions by the teacher. The teacher knows Devonta is bright because his answers are usually correct, but his seemingly impulsive and hyperactive behavior is distracting his classmates.

Devonta's Mom is advised by the school to consult her pediatrician for possible ADHD. The pediatrician requests Mom and the teacher to complete behavioral checklists for possible ADHD. In reviewing the checklists, the pediatrician notices the teacher's observations are different from those of Devonta's parents. The teacher observations do, indeed, suggest ADHD. But the parents' observations record normal behaviors at home. The pediatrician advises psychological testing.

The school psychologist completes a battery of tests, including IQ and Achievement tests and measures of Social Maturity. The results reveal Devanta's abilities at 6 years of age are equivalent to those of an eight year old. Attention span, problem-solving and language skills are all well above average. A recommendation is made to place Devonta into a gifted educational program.

Several months later, another set of ADHD checklists are completed by Devonta's parents and his new teacher. This time, both sets of observations are consistent and "normal". Devonta is happily performing at the third grade level, 2 years beyond his age.

What to ask before beginning to treat ADHD: **"What should my child be able to do when the disorder is effectively treated?"**

To answer this question, begin with an assessment of the child's physical health by a physician, then proceed to measures of the child's social and academic capabilities by a psychologist; finally, establish a measure of the child's current performance by the educators.

Expecting discipline to be effective for a child with untreated ADHD.

The core symptoms of ADHD include impulsivity (acting on thoughts without calculating likely consequences), distractibility (the flooding of consciousness with irrelevant thoughts and sensations) and inability to organize required steps to reach more distant goals. This means an affected child is unable to anticipate the consequences of behavior choices. Thus, ADHD blocks effective discipline. When an affected child's misbehavior fails to earn a reward or worse still, results in punishment, the child is surprised, even shocked.

Children don't choose to suffer with ADHD, and they can't choose to leave it behind. When children are punished for their inability to achieve appropriate behavioral goals, blocked by ADHD, their frustration leads to anger and depression.

ADHD is usually due to abnormal brain "wiring" or chemistry (often inherited), but occasionally may be caused by physical disturbances, such as exposure to toxins, gland disorders, unrecognized seizures and many other conditions, including emotional stress. Until underlying conditions such as these are recognized and treated with effective medication or psychotherapy, discipline cannot be effectively imposed.

What to ask before disciplining a child with ADHD: **"Has the ADHD been fully evaluated and effectively treated?"**

Failing to discipline children with effectively treated ADHD.

Discipline requires children to learn from the consequences of their acts. Arguably, the most disruptive symptom of untreated ADHD is children's inability to sequence and organize thoughts. To respond to discipline, children need to anticipate the predicted consequences of discipline.

ADHD, when effectively treated, restores an otherwise normal child's ability to perform at age level, so parents' expectations for appropriate discipline should also be restored to age equivalency. To put it most simply, once successfully treated, ADHD doesn't justify defiant behavior. Willful misbehavior requires and responds to appropriate forms of discipline.

Parents sometimes mistakenly accept misbehavior in a child with untreated ADHD as a character trait rather than a symptom of an untreated disorder. Successful treatment of the disorder, by eliminating barriers to their child's anticipation of consequences, provides an essential prerequisite for effective discipline.

What to ask once ADHD is effectively treated: **"Am I teaching my child to behave well by imposing meaningful consequences through discipline?"**

Treating ADHD only on schooldays.

ADHD is a life problem, not a school problem. A child's inability to think ahead to the consequences of chosen behaviors, carry out tasks with several successive steps and avoid dangerous acts places a child at risk in all settings, not just in school.

Besides these reasons for treating ADHD seven days a week, parents' observations over weekends as well as teachers' observations in school provide the prescribers of medication additional feedback regarding the effectiveness of treatment.

My recommendation to parents is to treat ADHD seven days a week.

Allowing one divorced parent to medicate and the other not to medicate.

Treatment routines with medication require a child's metabolism to adjust to the effects of medication. Erratic administration of medication makes such adjustments more difficult and creates metabolic stress. In addition, ADHD properly treated restores a child's performance capabilities, while withholding treatment curtails a child's performance. Children experiencing highs and lows in performance often choose a safer path of lower performance to avoid frustration and criticism.

What to ask before divorced parents elect to treat their child: **"Do we both agree our child has ADHD and requires**

treatment? Can we put aside our personal differences and act in unison for our child's sake?"

Failing to check a child for substance abuse.

Many illicit drugs can cause one or more of the symptoms of ADHD. For example, marijuana and cocaine can cause hyperactivity, racing thoughts and inability to organize tasks requiring successive steps – all symptoms shared with ADHD.

What to ask if your child could be exposed to or have access to illicit drugs: **"Has my child been tested for illicit drug use?"**

Common Errors Professionals Make with ADHD

Mistaking the mania of Bipolar Disorder for ADHD.

Bipolar disorder has historically been called Manic-Depressive disorder because those affected by the disorder exhibit waves of emotion ranging from the upward pole of hyperactivity, recklessness and irritability to the downward pole of sadness, depression, feelings of worthlessness and lack of motivation. When an affected child is seen during the upward or manic pole of bipolar disorder, ADHD may mistakenly be diagnosed. Over time, the distinction between bipolar disorder and ADHD will be made by most professionals. Errors in diagnosis are usually due to inadequate consult time with the professional.

What to ask if a professional consultant has spent only limited time with your child: **"Have you observed my child long enough to be sure we're not dealing with bipolar disorder?"**

Treating ADHD before treating a coexisting Mood Disorder.

Unstable mood or emotional instability is a condition found in many emotional disorders such as bipolar disorder, cyclothymic disorder, intermittent explosive disorder and many others. Any of these disorders may coexist with ADHD. Depending upon the choice of medication made by a professional to treat ADHD, mood instability may be worsened – sometimes to a catastrophic level.

One very common error made by less experienced professionals is to begin treating a child with bipolar disorder and ADHD with a stimulant medication before stabilizing emotion. An example will be instructive.

Vincent is treated by his Pediatrician for ADHD and frequent rages.

Vincent, age 9 years, is brought to his pediatrician after his mother receives repeated complaints from school regarding his inability to remain in his seat, his impulsive calling out in class and his tendency to rush through (and usually fail) tests. In addition, the teacher has complained Vincent has repeatedly broken pencils, torn up his papers and even overturned a desk in angry response to criticism or the imposition of limits.

Mom has already seen and discussed these observations with Vincent's pediatrician. The pediatrician advised her to have Vincent's teacher fill out a Vanderbilt Scale (designed to assess and rate the component symptoms of ADHD), documenting the teacher's observations in class. The pediatrician reviews the scale and, along with Mom's observations, concludes Vincent suffers from ADHD. Vincent is given a prescription for methylphenidate, a stimulant medication often used effectively to treat ADHD.

The next week, Mom calls the Pediatrician in a panic. Vincent has been suspended from school after stabbing another child with pencil during a rage. The teacher had sent Vincent to a time out area of the class after he hit a female classmate. Rather than going to time out, Vincent stabbed the girl in the arm with a pencil.

The pediatrician refers Vincent and his mother to a child psychiatrist. The psychiatrist confirms the pediatrician's diagnosis of ADHD, but adds a diagnosis of Mood Disorder. A mood stabilizing medication is prescribed with the methylphenidate. Over several weeks, the doses of both medications are adjusted until both ADHD and the mood disorder are under control. Vincent returns to class, able to perform his work adequately and without rages.

What to ask if your child's emotions are out of control when treatment is initiated for ADHD: **"Could my child have a mood disorder in addition to ADHD, requiring its own treatment?"**

Using too low a dose of stimulant medication to treat ADHD.

Another common error made by less experienced physicians treating ADHD is the use of too low a dose of medication to effectively control symptoms.

Some children are "fast metabolizers" of medication. Usually, these children have little or no response to usual doses of medication. That is, they neither respond adequately nor experience any ill effects from medication at usual doses because they eliminate the medication at a faster rate than normal. Most often, the observation of little or no response to medication extends to many different drugs, given for many different conditions, thus providing a clue to this condition. For example, higher than usual doses of anticonvulsants may be required to control epilepsy, higher doses of sedatives may be required to induce sleep and higher doses of stimulant medications may be required to control ADHD.

In general, "off label" use of medications at higher doses for ADHD are best left to behavioral specialists, like child psychiatrists, pediatric neurologists and behavioral-developmental pediatricians. Nonetheless, if a parent sees little or no response to medications prescribed for ADHD, consultation with a behavioral specialist may be the next step to take.

What to ask if your child neither responds to medication nor experiences any ill effects: **"Could my child be a 'fast metabolizer' requiring higher than usual doses of medication?"**

Delaying treatment of a child with disruption of critical life functions.

As you've learned in Chapter One, a "disorder" in childhood may be defined as a condition impinging on normal function. Left untreated, disorders disrupt life functions and may eventually lead to life-endangering consequences. You've learned normal function in childhood may be defined by three parameters. Each parameter must be exhibited consistently; that is, most of the time and in most places:

- Exhibiting physical, social and educational performance at levels consistent with ability.
- Abiding by reasonable rules.

- Getting along well enough with others that complaints from others are minimal and non-intrusive for the child and the child's family.

A child's inability to achieve normal function, caused by an untreated disorder, leads to frustration, anger or depression, behavioral problems and, eventually, rejection by others. Ultimately, outwardly directed aggression or inwardly directed self-injury will result.

I've often been asked, **"How early in life would you treat ADHD?"** The answer is, as early as abnormal function affects critical life functions. When love relationships are threatened at home, when acquisition of social or educational skills are falling well behind, when rule-breaking threatens ill health or injury and when rejection by peers, family and teachers becomes apparent, it's time to treat. When ADHD is the offending disorder, it's time to treat the ADHD.

Advising the treatment of ADHD with counseling alone.
ADHD is not acquired by design. That is, no child decides to suffer with ADHD. Likewise, no child can learn a strategy from a counselor to be rid of ADHD. Though it is true symptoms can be lessened by less distracting environments (like a quiet cubbyhole, preferential seating close to a teacher, one-on-one attention), placed in a "normal" distracting environment, a child with ADHD will suffer its effects on learning, rule-following and social relationships.

Counseling can be helpful for older children who have a degree of control over their environments. They can learn to find a quiet place to work, read while pacing or use other strategies acquired from a counselor. But only definitive treatment is able to equip a child to function in any environment, especially in younger age groups.

What to ask if your physician advises counseling alone: **"How will I measure the success of counseling and how long should it take? If it fails to improve my child's functioning, can you recommend a specialist for a second opinion?"**

Failing to arrange educational accommodations for ADHD.

The intrusiveness of ADHD symptoms and the severity of the disorder are greatly affected by the environment within which a child functions. In an isolated setting, where relationships to others are irrelevant, levels of performance are ignored and where safety is absolute, ADHD loses its designation as a "disorder." Other than within a padded time-out room, it's hard to envision such an environment. As expectations increase for a child's ability to demonstrate skills, abide by rules and relate to others, the impact of ADHD is magnified.

Many professionals treat ADHD with medication and counseling, but fail to suggest to educators simple steps to improve a child's school environment, such as allowing an affected child to take untimed tests, sit nearer the teacher or use a quiet cubbyhole free of distraction for routine academic tasks.

What to ask when a treatment plan is constructed for a child with ADHD: **"Have any plans been made in school to accommodate my child's disorder?"**

Now that we've examined some mistakes parents and professionals sometimes make in diagnosing and treating ADHD, let's learn a bit about the medications used to manage ADHD and associated conditions commonly seen with this condition.

Chapter Four

About medications used for ADHD & associated disorders

This chapter is written to acquaint parents with some of the more commonly used medications for the treatment of ADHD and associated mental health disorders. Generic and common brand name designations are both presented whenever possible. The chapter is not written to take the place of parents' professional consultants nor does it attempt to provide recipes for success. The author's goal is to provide parents a basic understanding of medication groups, common risks and potential benefits and the basis for meaningful discussion between parents and mental health professionals.

The discussion of medications in this chapter is not all-inclusive – new medications are constantly under investigation and are introduced periodically. The author holds the view that new medications, especially when used for children, are best prescribed cautiously or not at all until safety has been adequately determined. In most cases, the overall safety of a medication cannot be determined for several years and, in many cases, absolute safety can never be assured. Indeed, professional prescribers, especially in the case of children, routinely weigh the impact of untreated ADHD on critical life functions against the risks of using a particular medication. For most ADHD medications, parents are best advised to seek assistance from professionals with extensive experience treating ADHD.

The stimulant medications.

As you learned in the Introduction, ADHD, initially known as "A Defect in Moral Control," then designated "Minimal Brain Dysfunction" and finally "ADHD", was discovered by chance in the late 1930's to respond to Benzedrine, a stimulant medication then used to treat headaches and mucous congestion. The beneficial effect on hyperactivity, distractibility and impulsivity (all contributing to the "defect in moral control") lasted only four to six hours and was associated with dry mouth, increased pulse, increased blood pressure, occasional palpitations of the heart and decreased appetite. Some children exhibited excessive emotionality. When given at night, sleeplessness often occurred.

Over the years, researchers working with drug manufacturers have modified the chemical structure of this class of medications. The goal has been to increase the effectiveness and decrease or eliminate the side effects seen with Benzedrine. Nonetheless, all stimulant medications share these side effects to some degree. Since each child's metabolism differs subtly from every other child, individual responses and the occurrence of side effects differ from child to child as well. In this sense, the prescribing of a stimulant medication for a child with ADHD is an experiment unto itself.

Caution regarding reported side effects of ANY medication: cause vs. association.

Parents are often terrified by the length of the list of possible side effects for a medication prescribed by their doctors. Included in this list are all the horrible things reported to have occurred to people taking the medication. But, in many cases, worrisome events cannot be shown to have been caused by the medication. Rather, the events having occurred while the medication was being taken, can only be viewed as having been associated with the taking of the medication. For example, a rash might have been reported while a child took Ritalin. The rash might have been caused by the medication, but might also have been due to orange juice taken to swallow the tablet. This is why seeking a provider with experience prescribing the medication is so important. Such an experienced provider can accurately weigh risks against benefits.

In the following descriptions, the reader can safely assume all possible damaging events, including death, have been reported by someone at some time for each medication discussed. The author has limited summaries of side effects for each medication to those known to have been frequently caused by the medication. Such potential side effects must be weighed carefully against any hoped for benefit.

Here follow descriptions of stimulant medications commonly prescribed for ADHD. All stimulant medications may cause one or more of the following common side effects. When such side effects do occur, both parent and prescriber must decide if the side effect is intrusive or dangerous enough to warrant stopping the medication or whether the side effect can or should be tolerated when weighed against the benefit:

Common side effects of all stimulant medications.

- Emotion made more intense (like depression, anger, anxiety)
- Sleeplessness when active later in the day
- Decreased appetite, weight loss, low blood sugar (with irritability)
- Nausea, stomachache, headache
- Faster heart rate, knocking of the heart (palpitations), higher blood pressure
- Risk of irregular heart rate and sudden death in children with heart disease
- Jitteriness, worsened tics (involuntary muscle movements)
- Dry mouth
- Constipation

Methylphenidate (Metadate, Methylin, Ritalin).

This stimulant is available in many forms – liquid, chewable, tablet and capsule. It lasts 4 – 6 hours per dose. As a "controlled" substance (not a narcotic, like heroin, cocaine or codeine), its prescriptions are carefully monitored and prescriptions cannot be transmitted electronically. Instead, written prescriptions are required for each refill.

Pros: One of the gentlest of stimulants in its effects on emotions. This medication has been used for many years and its side effects have been well defined. It's also the least expensive of the stimulants and is therefore covered by most insurance plans.

Cons: Because methylphenidate works only 4 – 6 hours, it must typically be administered several times a day and in school this medication requires students to visit the school nurse for its administration.

Methylphenidate ER (Concerta, Metadate ER, Methylin ER, Ritalin LA, Ritalin S/R, Quillivant).

Extended release (ER) varieties of methylphenidate have been formulated to last during most or all of the day.

Pros: ER forms of methylphenidate are more convenient for all- day effectiveness. Quillivant is a liquid, long-acting form of methylphenidate. These forms of methylphenidate, depending upon a child's metabolism, may last 8 – 12 hours, or even longer.

Cons: Other than Quillivant, ER methylphenidate requires a child to swallow the pill or capsule without crushing or chewing it. This can be an obstacle for some children. Because some of the ER forms of methylphenidate last more than 12 hours, they may interfere with sleep. Sleep delay, as a side effect, must be weighed against the beneficial effects of the medication, and parents and prescribers may opt to add a nighttime sleep medication. The medication often suppresses appetite at lunchtime and may result in weight loss. Insurance plans don't always cover ER forms of methylphenidate.

Methylphenidate transdermal patch (Daytrana).

This form of methylphenidate is manufactured as a sticky patch containing enough of the medication to last approximately 9 hours. It is applied to the skin, usually the hip, 2 hours before the desired period of action and removed up to 9 hours later.

Pros: The extended period of action eliminates the need for in-school dosing. A steady release of the medication over most of the action period avoids "ups and downs" in its effect, lessening emotional instability and often allowing for a lower total dose of the medication than is required of pills or capsules.

Cons: Children with skin rash, such as psoriasis or eczema, are often unable to use this medication and rash at the patch sites is commonly encountered. Due to the delayed onset of action (up to 2 hours after the patch is applied), ADHD symptoms may be intrusive. Often, a "quick start" tablet of methylphenidate must be given as the patch is applied to control early morning symptoms. Insurance plans may not cover this designer drug.

Dexmethylphenidate tablets (Focalin).

This form of methylphenidate can be considered a modified version of methylphenidate. For some children, it is more effective at lower doses than methylphenidate, thus escaping some side effects.

Pros: Dexmethylphenidate may control ADHD symptoms in some children who fail to respond to methylphenidate. In my experience, this medication is less likely to intensify emotion than dextroamphetamine-containing stimulants.

Cons: Dexmethylphenidate shares the full list of possible side effects common to all stimulants. Insurance plans may not cover this medication.

Dexmethylphenidate capsules (Focalin XR – extended release).

As with the tablet form of this medication, some children may respond to lower doses than with methylphenidate. This extended release form of dexmethylphenidate may cover an 8 – 10 hour period.

Pros: Lower doses may be possible with this medication than with methylphenidate. In-school dosing may be eliminated.

Cons: Children must be able to swallow the capsules without crushing or chewing them. This can be an obstacle for some children. The medication often suppresses appetite at lunchtime and may result in weight loss. Insurance plans don't always cover dexmethylpphenidate capsules.

Dextroamphetamine tablets and liquid (Dexedrine, Zenzedi, ProCentra).

Dextroamphetamine is one of the earlier forms of stimulant medication. It is available as tablets and, as ProCentra, in liquid form. Single doses of the medication typically last 4 – 6 hours.

Pros: For some children, low doses may be more effective than higher doses of other stimulants. In generic form, it is usually covered by insurance plans.

Cons: Dextroamphetamine in any form has a high abuse potential. Risk of dependency is high in abusers of the drug and significant even in children appropriately treated for ADHD.

This medication almost always intensifies emotion – often causing anger flare ups, depression, anxiety or manic episodes. Dextroamphetamine should not be used with a large number of other medications. Prescribers must consider other medications a child is taking before prescribing dextroamphetamine.

Dextroamphetamine Spansules (Dexedrine - extended release capsules).

In spansule (extended release capsule) form, dextroamphetamine usually lasts an 8 hour period.

Pros: Extended release capsules may eliminate the need for multiple dosing or in-school administration.

Cons: Insurance plans may not cover spansules. If the medication lasts till evening hours, sleeplessness may result. Intensification of emotion, possible conflict with other medications a child may be taking, and dependency and abuse potential are considerations spansules share with tablet and liquid forms of dextroamphetamine. All common side effects listed above for stimulant medications are more prevalent with the use of this medication than with other stimulants.

Dextroamphetamine+Amphetamine tablets (Adderall).

This medication, a mixture of two stimulants, in my experience falls between dextroamphetamine and methylphenidate in the intensity of its common side effects. It's a more recent addition to the stimulant group than dextroamphetamine.

Pros: Tablets often last through an eight hour period, eliminating the need for more expensive extended release forms. The medication is also often more effective for hyperactivity (the "H" in ADHD) than methylphenidate, while having less intense an effect on emotion than dextroamphetamine.

Cons: When the medication lasts only 4 or 6 hours, multiple doses may be required, including administration at school. This stimulant, like dextroamphetamine, is a drug of potential abuse and may result in dependency, even in children who are appropriately treated for ADHD.

Dextroamphetamine+Amphetamine Spansules (Adderall XR capsules).

Dextroamphetamine+Amphetamine Spansules offer the convenience of once daily administration.

Pros: Medication effect often lasts till evening hours when administered early in the morning, thus giving parents the same behavioral benefits bestowed on teachers. The capsules can be sprinkled on applesauce or other food for children who cannot swallow capsules. This stimulant can often replace higher doses of methylphenidate while effectively controlling symptoms of ADHD.

Cons: The likelihood and intensity of the common side effects of stimulants listed above are often greater with this medication than with methylphenidate, especially appetite suppression, emotional instability and sleep delay. Insurance plans may not cover these spansules. As with tablets, dextroamphetamine+amphetamine spansules are a drug of potential abuse.

Lisdexamphetamine (Vyvanse capsules).
This stimulant is converted in the body to dextroamphetamine. It is designed to cover a 12 hour period.

Pros: Lisdexamphetamine usually works throughout the typical school day, eliminating the need for in-school administration.

Cons: Its active component, dextroamphetamine, may cause intensification of emotion, appetite suppression, sleeplessness and possible conflict with other medications a child may be taking. As with all stimulants, dependency and abuse potential are considerations this medication shares with tablet and liquid forms of dextroamphetamine. All common side effects listed above for stimulant medications have been encountered with the use of this medication.

The "stimulant" antidepressants.

Over the years, certain antidepressants have been found to lessen distractibility and improve concentration in some children with ADD, though they have little discernible effect on hyperactivity. Thus these medications may be a good fit for children with ADD with no hyperactivity, allowing lower doses of stimulants or even eliminating the need for stimulants entirely.

Bupropion hydrochloride (Wellbutrin, Wellbutrin S/R, XL, Budeprion, Buproban, Forfivo, Zyban).

Pros: This antidepressant, rather than intensifying emotions like depression, anxiety or anger as do stimulant medications, usually lessens depression and anxiety with little or no effect on anger. Unlike many antidepressants that increase appetite and excess weight gains, bupropion typically lessens appetite and often results in weight loss – a useful effect for overweight children.

The dual effects of this drug – lessening depression and anxiety while improving concentration – provide an attractive alternative to stimulant medication for children with milder forms of ADD.

Cons: In my experience, this antidepressant shares all the side effects listed for stimulant medications, though most are less common than with stimulants.

Potentially severe, though uncommon side effects include seizures and liver irritation. Like other antidepressants, bupropion may increase the risk of suicide. Worsening of some psychiatric disorders like bipolar disorder may occur. Blood pressure may be elevated and hypertension worsened.

Commonly encountered side effects include appetite suppression with weight loss and heart palpitations.

Venlafaxine (Effexor, Effexor XR).

Pros: This antidepressant offers the dual actions mentioned for bupropion above. It can be useful as an alternative to bupropion if the latter antidepressant fails to improve ADD symptoms.

Cons: In addition to the possibility of the side effects mentioned for bupropion above, venlafaxine may uncommonly cause Parkinson-like muscle movements, bleeding, liver or pancreas irritation, salt and water imbalance, severe rash, pneumonia and glaucoma.

As with all medications prescribed for the management of ADHD, consultation with an experienced physician who can competently weigh the pros and cons of these antidepressants is a critical part of the treatment strategy.

Antidepressant-like medication

Atomoxetine (Strattera).

This medication is in a class of its own. It is used to improve ADD symptoms and rarely, if ever, improves hyperactivity. In its actions and side effects, it most closely resembles the "stimulant" antidepressants.

Pros: Unlike the stimulants and stimulant antidepressives, atomoxetine rarely causes appetite suppression or weight loss. Its duration of action allows most children to take the medication once a day, either in the morning or at bedtime.

Cons: Side effects with this medication are uncommon, but when they occur, they can be severe. They include many potential ill effects on the heart, especially in children with pre-existing heart problems, risk of seizures, risk of suicide and worsening of psychiatric illness like bipolar disorder and mood disturbances. Other rare occurrences include liver irritation, severe rash and wide swings in blood pressure.

"Calming" medications

Some medications have been found useful for controlling hyperactivity, the "H" part of ADHD, though they have little or no effect on focus or concentration, the ADD parts of ADHD. Both medications listed have other effects as well and these effects can be considered side effects, though for some children they may be beneficial.

Clonidine (Catapres, Kapvay).

This medication has a long history of use as a blood pressure-lowering agent.

Pros: Clonidine has been found effective for calming the hyperactivity and impulsivity and occasionally the distractibility of ADHD. It avoids most of the potential ill effects of stimulants and stimulant antidepressants. It is sometimes effective in controlling muscle and vocal tics (Motor tics: repetitive muscle twitches which may be "simple" as with eye blinking or "complex", involving a series of muscle movements of a repetitive nature – like rubbing an item, then sniffing it. Vocal tics: sounds, words or phrases uttered repetitively). Tourette Disorder and Restless Leg Syndrome are examples of disorders which may be responsive to Clonidine. For children with both a Tic Disorder and ADHD, clonidine may be considered a preferred medication.

Cons: Side effects are frequent and some are potentially serious. These include decreased alertness, fatigue, depression, heart rhythm problems, low blood pressure, even sudden death in individuals with pre-existing heart disease.

Guanfacine (Tenex, Intuniv).

Guanfacine belongs to the same group of medications as Clonidine, discussed above. As such, it shares the potential side effects listed under Clonidine. This medication has long been used to stabilize mood (emotional instability) in many psychiatric disorders and has also been used to control high blood pressure. Like Clonidine above, Guanfacine is often effective for calming the hyperactivity and impulsivity and occasionally the distractibility of ADHD. It, too, avoids most of the potential ill effects of stimulants and stimulant antidepressants. It may help to control muscle and vocal tics (Motor tics: repetitive muscle twitches which may be "simple" as with eye blinking or "complex", involving a series of muscle movements of a repetitive nature – like rubbing an item, then sniffing it. Vocal tics: sounds, words or phrases uttered repetitively). Tourette Disorder and Restless Leg Syndrome are examples of disorders which may respond to Clonidine. For children with both a Tic Disorder and ADHD, Guanfacine, like Clonidine, may be considered a preferred medication1.

Pros: Guanfacine may calm the hyperactivity, impulsivity and occasionally the distractibility of ADHD. It avoids most of the potential ill effects of stimulants and stimulant antidepressants. It is sometimes effective in controlling motor and vocal tics.

Cons: Side effects like fatigue and decreased alertness are common, especially with higher doses. More serious side effects may occur and include depression, heart rhythm problems, low blood pressure, and even sudden death in individuals with pre-existing heart disease.

Buspirone (Buspar).

Buspirone is a unique anxiety/aggression-reducing antidepressant. Its precise mode of action is incompletely understood. In recent years, besides its usefulness as a treatment for anxiety/aggression, it has been prescribed for ADHD, especially when side effects have been encountered with more commonly used medications.

Pros: Unlike stimulant medications, Buspirone is not a drug of abuse and does not promote dependence (its use can be stopped without symptoms of physical withdrawal.) It can be especially useful when anxiety or aggression coexist with ADHD.

Cons: Buspirone is not as reliably effective as stimulant medications in managing ADHD.

Now that we know a bit about the history, the symptoms and the treatment of the disorder currently recognized as Attention Deficit (Hyperactivity), we might ask, How do we know when to stop treating ADHD? In the next chapter, we learn to answer this question with a simple test.

References:

1. Am J Psychiatry. 2001 Jul;158(7):1067-74

Chapter Five

When can we stop treating ADHD?

In Chapter One we learned to suspect a disorder when we observe a pattern of abnormal behavior. As parents, we learned abnormal behavior in a child could be defined by applying three criteria to any observed behavior. We could ask ourselves and those with authority over a child if the child is:

- Performing critical life functions at a level consistent with ability.
- Abiding by reasonable rules.
- Getting along well enough with others that complaints from others are minimal and non-intrusive for the child and the child's family.

A child who consistently performs normally in accomplishing critical life functions, abides by reasonable rules and relates peacefully with others does not have the disorder of ADH and requires no treatment.

It's true that a child (or an adult, for that matter) who is "flighty and fidgety," but is consistently meeting each of the above-mentioned criteria, may have ADH, but the last D (disorder) does not apply. ADH may determine who befriends that child and later, who marries that adult, but such an idiosyncrasy does not warrant medical treatment.

In my experience, the treatment of a disorder should end when a child sustains normal performance during a trial without treatment.

What is normal performance? Achievement vs. ability.

You might think anyone could recognize normal performance in a child, especially professionals. But the fact is, many children who no longer exhibit a disorder continue to be treated unnecessarily because many parents and some professionals fail to compare a child's level of achievement with the child's ability.

Here's the difference between achievement and ability. Achievement is what a child has been observed to do. Ability is what a child is capable of doing. Anyone, including parents and teachers, can observe a child's level of achievement. But, to define normal performance, an observer must decide which of two measures to use. One measure is to compare a child's level of achievement to that of most children of the same age or school grade level. The other measure of normal is to compare a child's performance to that child's ability level (or intelligence level). A child's intelligence must be measured by a qualified professional, usually a child psychologist. The two measures of normal performance for a child – achievement vs. ability - can be vastly different.

Some parents consider any discrepancy between their child's performance and the child's level of ability a disorder, even when the child's level of performance is average or above average for age. High expectations by parents can be highly motivating for some children, but for others, such expectations can be stressful enough to create their own disorder.

Other parents are content to accept average performance for age as a sufficient level of achievement, even when their child's ability far exceeds such performance.

Neither a definition of normal performance based on average-for-age achievement nor a definition of normal as achieving at ability level can be considered invariably correct. Each approach is best for some children, though treatment for ADHD may appropriately be withheld in one instance and not in the other.

Let's look at a couple of examples.

"Vertical" vs. "horizontal" measures of performance.

Maxine's prenatal development was normal as was her physical health during her first 3 years of life. Her developmental milestones were all achieved precociously. After 3 years of age, her parents had to change nursery schools and pre-kindergarten several times due to teachers' complaints of Maxine's high activity level, difficulty following directions and wandering. At 5 years of age, Maxine was diagnosed with ADHD and between 5 and 8 years of age, she was treated for ADHD and did well. Last year, her parents and her pediatrician decided to stop treating her ADHD. Maxine had matured and, with provision for preferential seating in class and a cubbyhole for her to work without distraction, she did well in an average 4th grade class.

Maxine is now 10 years old and this year her parents enrolled her in a 5th grade gifted program. She has a recently measured IQ of 130. The psychologist who performed the IQ tests advised Maxine's parents their daughter was easily capable of working at the 6th grade level and the parents decided to enroll her in advanced classes this year. She and her classmates are expected to perform between a 6th and 7th grade level. Lately, Maxine's parents have received several reports from her teachers complaining of disruptive behaviors, similar to those seen in earlier years. These behaviors were not seen last year in her "average" 4th grade class.

The teachers observe Maxine has difficulty focusing on her work, especially in math. She often wanders about in class, distracting other students. She frequently blurts out answers when other students are asked to respond.

Maxine's pediatrician provides her parents with an ADHD Diagnostic Teacher Rating Scale, which her parents and teachers complete. The scales completed at school are highly suggestive of ADHD. A similar scale completed by the parents at home does not suggest ADHD.

The parents ask their pediatrician if Maxine should resume treatment for ADHD. The pediatrician recognizes the most appropriate steps to take depend on the choice of performance vs. ability as a measure of a disorder. In describing this distinction, the doctor explains Maxine could use her superior intelligence to advance above her age range (vertical achievement) as the parents intended this year. In this case, many of Maxine's classmates would be older than she and might possess a greater level of maturity than she. Alternatively, Maxine might use her intellectual abilities to participate in a greater than average number of extracurricular activities at her own age level, though in greater depth (horizontal achievement).

The pediatrician advises the parents to present these choices to Maxine and explains treatment for ADHD might be again be indicated for the higher functioning curriculum – vertical achievement.

The parents choose to go for vertical performance - and treat ADHD.

After some discussion, Maxine's parents decide to keep their daughter in the gifted program. They do not feel 10 year old Maxine should be allowed to decide this issue. They request the pediatrician to resume treating Maxine's ADHD.

Unfortunately, the stimulant medication which was effective in the past and which caused no observable ill effects results in excessive weight loss, irritability and frequent crying episodes. Trials of other stimulant medications fare no better. Two non-stimulant medications do improve Maxine's focus, academic performance and rule-following, but their use prompts the parents to reconsider and follow through with the pediatrician's initial advice to discuss options with Maxine. Maxine embraces a return to her former classmates in the average 5th grade class while her parents construct supplemental extracurricular activities for their daughter.

Maxine chooses horizontal performance – without treatment for ADHD.

With Maxine's request to return to her grade level classes, her pediatrician authorizes preferential seating in class and provision of a quiet workplace for Maxine, as was effective in the past. She suggests a trial off medication and she and the parents are gratified to observe Maxine continues to perform and behave well off her medications.

Discussion:

Since Maxine's academic ability level is that of a 13 year old (as defined by her IQ level), her performance at the 5th grade level, 3 years below her level of ability, could be considered deficient. The pediatrician knew treating Maxine's ADHD symptoms of impulsivity, hyperactivity and poor focus would likely improve her performance in her gifted academic program. Treating a discrepancy of 3 years between achievement level and ability level was an example of the use of vertical performance as a measure of a disorder.

Maxine's academic performance at the 10 year level easily met the "average" 5th grade level of achievement. In that sense, using this horizontal measure of performance, along with acceptable behavior, eliminated any criteria for a disorder.

Had Maxine expressed disappointment at being unable to perform well in a gifted program, a case could have been made for treatment, even when several medications were required. However, since she was happier and better adjusted in the average classroom, treating her for ADHD was unnecessary and unwise.

The triggering of Maxine's ADHD symptoms in a stressful setting and their disappearance in a less stressful setting underscores the impact of environment on disorders of all varieties, including ADHD.

Next, let's look at the example of Stewart, an intellectually impaired child with undiagnosed ADHD.

Effect of treatment vs. non-treatment of ADHD on measures of ability.

Stewart is 8 years old. During his mother's pregnancy, both parents were heavy alcohol and cocaine users. Stewart suffered seizures as an infant and later as a toddler. He exhibited delayed milestones by 8 months of age and at 1 year of age he was removed from his parents' care and placed in foster care, then adopted by his foster parents. At 4 years of age, Stewart was diagnosed and treated for ADHD. By 5 years of age on entry into kindergarten and with improvement in hyperactivity, medication was stopped.

Stewart is now enrolled in a 1st grade class, having repeated kindergarten, then 1st grade last year. He cannot complete his assignments His behavior is characterized by wandering in class, "hyperactivity", described as touching everything in sight, scribbling on his desk and on the walls and inability to follow even simple directions. Stewart cries easily and often has violent temper outbursts when disciplined for these behaviors. His teacher asks the parents to have him evaluated by his pediatrician.

Stewart's parents are advised by his pediatrician to schedule formal psychological testing, including measures of IQ, achievement, social maturity and emotional responsiveness. The parents elect to have these tests done by the school psychologist at Stewart's home school, thus avoiding expense.

The school psychologist meets with Stewart's parents to review test results. She explains the tests have revealed 8 year old Stewart's overall abilities are equivalent to those of a 5 year old (overall IQ of 65) and that his enrollment in a first grade class, where his classmates are working at the 6 year level, is beyond his capabilities. In reviewing the many parts of the IQ test, the psychologist relates she noticed Stewart's performance was poorest when he was given a limited period of time to complete a task. On untimed parts of the testing, Stewart did better. Indeed, the psychologist reported, had Stewart done as well on timed tests as he did on untimed tests, his overall performance would have been equal to that of a 6 ½ year old. At that level, Stewart would likely succeed with his enrollment in 1st grade this year.

The parents review a copy of the psychological tests with their pediatrician. The pediatrician recognizes a pattern of subtest scores suggestive of ADHD and, along with teacher observations provided by Stewart's parents, confirms the diagnosis ADHD. She recommends resuming treatment with a stimulant medication.

Several weeks after restarting medication, Stewart's behavior in class is dramatically improved. Even more gratifying is an upturn in Stewart's academic performance to the 6 ½ year level which, though below age norms for an 8 year old, is now apparently higher than that predicted by the recent IQ test. The parents and teacher complete ADHD Diagnostic Rating Scales with Stewart on medication, documenting the disappearance of a "disorder."

The pediatrician suggests repeating Stewart's IQ test on medication. Her recommendation is based on the fact that an IQ of 65 qualifies as Mild Mental Retardation, whereas Stewart's performance on medication is no longer in that range, qualifying instead as low normal functioning. Repeat psychological testing on medication yields an overall IQ of 81, highlighting the negative impact of untreated ADHD on measures of intelligence.

Discussion:

This scenario is very common, yet often misinterpreted by parents and professionals alike.

IQ testing is often accepted as a definitive measure of a child's ability. Yet, its accuracy is affected by any active disorder, including ADHD. In this scenario, Stewart's parents are fortunate to have chosen an experienced psychologist to do the testing. She is able to guide them away from accepting an inaccurate designation of Mild Mental Retardation. Had the parents accepted that level of ability for Stewart, the school would likely have placed Steward back in a kindergarten class.

Another important principle illustrated by Stewart's vignette is ADH acquires its last "D" - disorder - only in certain environments, but not in others. In many kindergartens, children are taught rules of peaceful coexistence with classmates, but not necessarily much in the way of academic learning. The focus often changes dramatically in 1st grade, where more complex learning is expected. As in Stewart's case, ADH, a mere annoyance in kindergarten, may morph into ADHD, requiring appropriate treatment.

Now that you've travelled through the complexities of ADHD – suspecting it, diagnosing it, managing it, putting its treatment to rest – let's summarize what you've learned.

Chapter Six

ADHD in a Nutshell

If you suspect your child has ADHD, check first for a disorder.

Begin by examining the criteria for the last "D" – disorder – in ADHD. If your child is performing normally in the following 3 areas, you can eliminate disorders, including ADHD:

- Performing critical life functions-
  - o Physical control of body functions (strength, stamina, eating, elimination) at a level appropriate for age.
  - o Benefitting from and enjoying Social interactions with others.
  - o Exhibiting comprehension and Educational performance consistent with age.
- Complying with reasonable rules.
- Coexisting with others without generating a pattern of complaints.

Remember, as you learned in the last chapter, normal performance can be measured "horizontally" by comparing your child's physical, social or educational performance to the average performance of children of the same age, or "vertically" against your child's measured ability level. Of these two measures, horizontal comparisons are least stressful and are least likely to define a disorder.

If your child is failing to perform normally, ADHD may be present.

There are many possible causes for a child's deficient performance in critical life functions, rule following and getting along with others. Many physical and mental health disorders can mimic ADHD. Some of these conditions, like Bipolar Disorder, Epilepsy, Hyperthyroidism and lead poisoning may cause progressive mental deterioration or nervous system damage if undetected. Professional consultation is mandatory to hone in on a specific diagnosis.

I have found using affected areas of critical life functions (physical, social, educational) as guides to appropriate consultants extremely useful:

- When physical deficiency is observed, consult a physician. Pediatricians and Behavioral-Developmental Pediatricians are best trained to begin looking for causes.
- When social or educational deficiency is encountered, consult a child psychologist. Child psychologists range in training from bachelor to doctorate levels. A child's home public school is a good first place to begin an evaluation. Child psychologists can perform tests of intelligence, achievement level, social maturity and emotional reactivity. They can offer counselling and therapy.
- When educational performance must be monitored over time to assess the success or

failure of treatment, Educators (like teachers, speech and language specialists, occupational therapists) are best equipped to provide ongoing observations.

If ADHD is diagnosed, consult an experienced physician.

Pediatricians, Behavioral-Developmental Pediatricians and Child Psychiatrists are trained to diagnose and treat ADHD.

Remember, environment plays a big part in determining the presence or absence of any disorder, including ADHD. This means when teachers, classes, schools or family dynamics change dramatically, the presence or absence of a disorder can also change.

Remember too, ADHD is not a willful disorder. This means its presence or absence and its impact on a child's performance cannot be controlled by motivation alone. Thus, discipline cannot obliterate ADHD. Ultimately, ADHD is an expression of abnormal brain chemistry and requires treatment of brain chemistry to be effectively managed.

ADHD affects all aspects of a child's life – critical life functions, rule following and relationships to others. Thus, ADHD must be considered a life disorder, not merely a school disorder. It's almost always best to treat ADHD 7 days a week.

Since each child's metabolism is unique, each child's response to medication is unique. Some children are fast metabolizers and require higher than usual doses of medication to effectively treat ADHD. Average or recommended dose ranges may not apply to some children.

It's for this reason parents must consult physicians experienced in the treatment of this disorder.

When teachers, classes, schools or family dynamics change, consider a trial without treatment.

Recalling the importance of environment in exposing symptoms of ADHD, be open to a carefully monitored trial off medication.

It's sometimes helpful to begin a medication-free trial on weekends when parents can directly observe performance. If a disorder re-emerges on weekends off medication, it's a certainty the disorder will re-emerge in school. If performance off medication remains acceptable on weekends, extending the trial to school is the next step.

Educators are best positioned to track performance off medication. To assist in organizing observations, ADHD Diagnostic Rating Scales for parents and teachers are available for download from the internet.

Suggested resources for additional information follow below.

General Information.

- www.adhd.com/

- http://www.nimh.nih.gov/health/topics/attention-deficit-hyperactivity-disorder-adhd/index.shtml

- http://www.cdc.gov/ncbddd/adhd/treatment.htm

- www.chadd.org/

- Taking Charge of ADHD, Third Edition: The Complete, Authoritative Guide for Parents, R. A. Barkley, Guilford Press, 2013

• Managing Misbehavior in Kids: The MIS/Kidding Process, A.M. Davick, 2014

ADHD Rating Scales for Parents and Teachers.

•http://www.brightfutures.org/mentalhealth/pdf/professionals/bridges/adhd.pdf

•http://psychcentral.com/addquiz.htm?gclid=Cj0KEQiAneujBRDcvL6f5uybhdABEiQA_ojMgg7ZFFQRN1nNggebYlvXc5DBJh7kJaoeWVt0clfPL7waAk2G8P8HAQ

About medications.

•http://www.webmd.com/add-adhd/guide/adhd-medication-chart

•http://www.drugs.com/condition/attention-deficit-disorder.html

•ADD/ADHD, A. Farrar, Lerner Publishing Group, 2010

•ADHD Solved, R. Patton, 2014

About the Author

Dr. Alan Davick, a Developmental-Behavioral Pediatrician, has taught parents and professional colleagues how to recognize and manage complex misbehavior in children for 40 years. Trained at the Johns Hopkins Medical Institutions, Dr. Davick has maintained clinical practice throughout those years. He has, as a Major in the Army Medical Corps, served as Pediatrician-in-Chief at Tuttle Army Health Clinic, Savannah GA and later, while engaged in private Pediatric practice, as Behavioral-Developmental Consultant to the Chatsworth School for Exceptional Children, in Baltimore County, MD.

Dr. Davick has focused his knowledge and experience on separating innate conditions like ADHD, Bipolar Disorder, Cerebral Palsy, Developmental Delay and Epilepsy, masquerading as willful misbehavior, from truly volitional misconduct, like Oppositional-Defiant Disorder and Conduct Disorders.

Dr. Davick lives with his wife, Barbara, in Cape Coral, FL, where he practices Child Psychiatry.

Ordering Information

For more information about Dr. Davick's books, please send your queries to:

Alan M. Davick, M.D.
MISKIDDING, LLC
P.O. Box 101127
Cape Coral, FL 33910-1127
URL: www.DrDavick.com
Email: miskidding1@gmail.com

Books by Dr. Alan M. Davick

- Managing Misbehavior in Kids: The Miskidding® Process
- Discipline Your Child without Going to Jail
- Bullying: Rarely Travels Alone
- ADHD: What Every Parent Should Know

Made in the USA
Middletown, DE
25 May 2019